THE NEXT GOAT

COCO GAUFF

CORINA JEFFRIES

PowerKiDS press

Published in 2025 by The Rosen Publishing Group, Inc.
2544 Clinton Street, Buffalo, NY 14224

First Edition

Editor: Greg Roza
Book Design: Rachel Rising

Photo Credits: Cover Victor Velter/Shutterstock.com; Cover, pp. 1, 3, 4, 6, 8, 10, 12, 14, 16, 18, 20, 22, 23, 24 Pixacon/Shutterstock.com; Cover Farhanz9/Shutterstock.com; Cover, p.1 Alhovik/Shutterstock.com; p. 4 grey_and/Shutterstock.com; pp. 5, 7, 21 lev radin/Shutterstock.com; p. 8 OrangeVector/Shutterstock.com; pp. 9, 15 Leonard Zhukovsky/Shutterstock.com; p. 11 David Collingwood / Alamy Stock Photo; p. 13 Rena Schild/Shutterstock.com; p. 17 Remo_Designer/Shutterstock.com; p. 18 Independent Photo Agency / Alamy Stock Photo; p. 18 Pixel-Shot/Shutterstock.com; p. 19 Action Plus Sports Images / Alamy Stock Photo.

Library of Congress Cataloging-in-Publication Data

Names: Jeffries, Corina, author.
Title: Coco Gauff / Corina Jeffries.
Description: Buffalo : PowerKids Press, [2025] | Series: The next GOAT | Includes index.
Identifiers: LCCN 2024033232 (print) | LCCN 2024033233 (ebook) | ISBN 9781499449709 (library binding) | ISBN 9781499449693 (paperback) | ISBN 9781499449716 (ebook)
Subjects: LCSH: Gauff, Coco, 2004–Juvenile literature. | Women tennis players–United States–Biography–Juvenile literature. | African American tennis players–Biography–Juvenile literature. | Tennis players–Rating of–United States–Juvenile literature. | Tennis–United States–History–Juvenile literature.
Classification: LCC GV994.G38 J44 2025 (print) | LCC GV994.G38 (ebook) | DDC 796.342092 [B]–dc23/eng/20240720
LC record available at https://lccn.loc.gov/2024033232
LC ebook record available at https://lccn.loc.gov/2024033233

Manufactured in the United States of America

CPSIA Compliance Information: Batch #CWPK25. For Further Information contact Rosen Publishing at 1-800-237-9932.

CONTENTS

MEET COCO!

Coco Gauff is one of the most exciting young **athletes** in sports today. At just 20 years old, Gauff has reached the rank of second best in the word in women's singles and number one in woman's doubles. She made a name for herself in tennis at age 15 by beating her **idol**, Venus Williams.

Gauff is a young, **determined** athlete. She's sure to keep making headlines with her natural talent and hard work. She just might be the next GOAT!

This is a photo of Gauff on her way to victory at the 2023 U.S. Open.

GROWING UP

Cori Dionne "Coco" Gauff was born in Atlanta, Georgia, on March 13, 2004. Her father, Corey Gauff, and her mother, Candi Gauff, are both athletes who had played **Division I** college sports. Coco has two younger brothers—Cameron and Codey.

Gauff was six years old when she became interested in tennis. The Gauffs decided to leave Atlanta and move to Delray Beach and spend time working on Coco's tennis skills. Corey quit his job to be Coco's coach. Candi quit her job to homeschool her.

WHAT THEY'RE SAYING

When she was only about 5 years old, Coco and her father were watching Serena Williams play in the Australian Open on televison. Corey called Serena the GOAT. When Corey told Coco it meant the greatest of all time, she said, "I want to be a GOAT!"

The Gauff family moved to Delray Beach because the area is well known for its tennis training centers.

RISING STAR

Gauff's father made sure she played several sports to make her a well-rounded athlete. In addition to tennis, Gauff tried basketball, soccer, gymnastics, and track.

When Gauff was 10, she went to France to train under famous coach Patrick Mouratoglou. This training helped Gauff improve greatly. In 2014, Gauff won the U.S. Tennis Association Clay Court National 12-and-under title. In 2017, Gauff came in second during the U.S. Open Girls Junior **Championship**. In 2018, when she was just 14, Gauff won the French Open junior championship.

Gauff's serves are tough to return. They have been measured at more than 120 miles (193 km) per hour!

BEATING VENUS

Gauff wowed fans in 2019 by becoming the youngest woman to earn a spot at the Wimbledon Championships in London, England. The 15-year-old's first match was against one of her tennis idols—Venus Williams. Williams was 39 at the time, and had already won many championships, including five previous Wimbledon Championships.

Gauff beat Venus in two sets to move on in the **tournament**! In fact, she made it to the 4th round before losing. She became the youngest woman to reach this level since Jennifer Capriati did in 1991.

WHAT THEY'RE SAYING

"I was just telling her 'thank you' for everything she's done for the sport. She's been an **inspiration** for many people. I was just really telling her 'thank you'."

—Coco Gauff on speaking with Venus Williams after their Wimbledon match.

Gauff cheers after winning her first Wimbledon match against Venus Williams.

ALWAYS IMPROVING

Gauff's play in her first Grand Slam tournament showed that she was ready to compete with other players from around the world. The Grand Slam tournaments—also called majors—include the Australian Open, the French Open, Wimbledon, and the U.S. Open.

Although Gauff failed to win a Grand Slam tournament, she won several tournaments in the United States. This included the Billie Jean King Cup **qualifying** match in 2023 between the U.S Tennis team and Austria's team held in her hometown of Delray Beach. The U.S team beat Austria 4 games to 0.

WHAT THEY'RE SAYING

"Coco is a special one. She loves the big stage, is very well prepared on and off the court, and—most importantly—she knows there are so many more opportunities [chances] ahead for her life and her career."

—U.S. tennis great Billie Jean King

This photograph shows Gauff and her doubles teammate Caty McNally after winning the Citi Open tournament in Washington, D.C., on August 3, 2019.

2023 U.S. OPEN

Gauff made it to the final match of the 2022 French Open but lost to Polish player Iga Świątek. Gauff said she watched Świątek lift the trophy, or prize, thinking, "I want to feel what that felt like for her."

In 2023, 19-year-old Gauff made it to the final round of the U.S. Open against Belarusian player Aryna Sabalenka. Sabalenka had won the Australian Open earlier in the year. Gauff lost the first set, but she came back to win the next two. She had won her first Grand Slam.

WHAT THEY'RE SAYING

"You have Coco, being now a Grand Slam winner, you can feel that she has more **confidence** in her game and her ability to win majors. So, this is going to be exciting."

—Patrick Mouratoglou, Gauff's former coach

Gauff's win at the 2023 U.S. Open as a teenager put her in good company. Tracy Austin won the 1979 U.S. Open when she was 16. Serena Williams won the U.S. Open in 1999 when she was 17.

2024 FRENCH OPEN

Entering the 2024 French Open, Gauff was listed as the number-three women's tennis player in the world. Everyone was expecting greatness, including Gauff herself.

Gauff made it through five rounds, losing only one match in the quarterfinal round (last eight players). She looked ready to win it all. She met number-one ranked Iga Świątek in the semifinal round (last four players). Gauff lost to Świątek in two sets.

While Gauff failed to win a second singles major, she wasn't done yet!

Gauff shakes hands with Iga Świątek after their match at the 2024 French Open.

DOUBLES CHAMP!

Gauff has had success in doubles matches. At a 2022 tournament in Toronto, Canada, Gauff teamed up with fellow American Jessica Pegula. They won the doubles final, making Gauff the number-one-ranked doubles player in the world.

At the 2024 French Open, Gauff teamed up with Katerina Siniaková of the Czech Republic. Gauff and Siniaková beat a team of Italian players in two sets. This was Gauff's second Grand Slam win in two years.

Gauff and Siniaková both lift the trophy for the women's doubles final on June 9, 2024.

WHAT'S NEXT?

In 2023, Gauff made nearly $23 million. This made her the highest-paid female athlete in the world! She has deals with companies such as New Balance (clothing and sneakers).

In 2020, Gauff was prepared to compete at the Olympic Games in Tokyo, Japan. However, she tested positive for the COVID-19 virus and had to back out. Gauff was selected first to be part of the 2024 U.S. Olympic Tennis Team. It's clear that Coco Gauff has the skill and drive to become the next GOAT.

WHAT THEY'RE SAYING

"She's fearless. We need some leaders in the women's game. She definitely will be one of them. If not *the* one."

—Chris Evert, tennis champion (18 women's major titles)

Coco poses with the trophy for winning the 2023 U.S. Open. Is this just the first of many Grand Slam wins for Gauff? Only time will tell!

GLOSSARY

athlete: A person who is trained in or good at games and exercises that require physical skill, endurance, and strength.

championship: A contest to find out who's the best player or team in a sport.

confidence: Belief in one's abilities.

determined: Not weak or uncertain.

Division I: The highest level of college sports in the United States.

idol: A greatly loved and admired person or thing.

inspiration: Something or someone that moves others to act.

qualify: In sports, to play well enough to make it to the next level.

tournament: A contest or series of contests played for a championship.

FOR MORE INFORMATION

BOOKS

Hansen, Grace. *Coco Gauff: Major Tennis Champion*. Minneapolis, MN: Abdo Kids Jumbo, 2024.

Zabel, Jimmy. *Coco Gauff Biography for Kids*. Independently Published, 2023.

WEBSITES

Coco Gauff
www.biography.com/athlete/coco-gauff
Read more about Coco Gauff here.

Women's Tennis Association (WTA)
www.wtatennis.com
Learn more about women's tennis and the tournaments it supports, as well as women athletes.

Publisher's note to educators and parents: Our editors have carefully reviewed these websites to ensure that they are suitable for students. Many websites change frequently, however, and we cannot guarantee that a site's future contents will continue to meet our high standards of quality and educational value. Be advised that students should be closely supervised whenever they access the internet.

INDEX